LEWIS C

WILD FLOWERS
of FOREST *&* WOODLAND
IN THE PACIFIC NORTHWEST

Written and photographed by
Lewis J. Clark

Edited by
John Trelawny

H A R B O U R   P U B L I S H I N G

Published by

HARBOUR PUBLISHING
P.O. Box 219
Madeira Park, BC Canada
V0N 2H0
www.harbourpublishing.com

Originally published: Sidney, B.C., Gray's Publishing, 1974
Cover photo: Large white trillium by William Merilees
Cover and interior design by Martin Nichols
Printed and bound in Canada

Harbour Publishing acknowledges the financial support of the Government of Canada through the Book Publishing Industry Development Program (BPIDP) and the Canada Council for the Arts, and the Province of British Columbia through the British Columbia Arts Council, for its publishing activities.

THE CANADA COUNCIL | LE CONSEIL DES ARTS
FOR THE ARTS | DU CANADA
SINCE 1957 | DEPUIS 1957

National Library of Canada Cataloguing in Publication Data

Clark, Lewis J., 1907–1974.
    Wild flowers of forest & woodland in the Pacific Northwest/
Lewis J. Clark; editor, John G.S. Trelawny.

    Includes index.
    Previous ed. has title: Lewis Clark's field guide to wild flowers of forest & woodland in the Pacific Northwest.
    ISBN 1-55017-306-5

    1. Wild flowers—Northwest, Pacific—Identification. 2. Forest plants—Northwest, Pacific—Identification. I. Trelawny, John G. S., 1919– II. Clark, Lewis J., 1907–1974. Lewis Clark's field guide to wild flowers of forest & woodland in the Pacific Northwest. III. Title.
QK110.C548 2003   582.13'09795'09152   C2003-910374-9

Introduction

Plants, like people, choose different places in which to live. Some plants (like some individuals) are able to adapt to a variety of habitats. But other plants demand a rather narrow range of light and shade, of soil porosity and acidity, of climatic factors—such as temperature minima, or of amount and distribution of rainfall. Hence though many, or most, of the plants described and pictured in this book are generally found in woodlands, or forests, some also occur on wet stream banks, or even on roadsides. The wanderer in shaded woods—dry or moist, deciduous or coniferous, near the sea or just below the timberline—will find in this book nearly all of the plants that may be discovered. But limitations of space have sometimes required that a woodland plant, if it is a species that lives and thrives in several habitats, must be described, for example, in the book on flowers of field and slope, or of sea coast, or of mountains. So if a plant one finds in the forest is not in this book, it may be a species that is happy also in wet ditches, or at high altitudes, or by the sea—and should be sought in the corresponding volumes of this series.

In terms of geographic range, wild flowers included in the series are the more common and showy plants that occur from southern Alaska, through British Columbia, Washington and Oregon, to northern California, from the coast to the western timberline of the Rockies.

Plants of woodland and forest associations obviously are able to grow in shade, but on closer examination one finds that there are varying degrees of shade. When an ancient tree of the forest falls, an opening is created into which more sunlight can penetrate. In such places will be found a particular group of species that is quite different from those growing in the deep gloom of the unbroken coniferous forest. Again, in woodlands of deciduous trees—such as maple or alder—much more light reaches the ground in early spring, before the leafy canopy develops. Here the searcher will find such plants as toothwort and yellow wood violet, which rush into early flower. But these are likely to be accompanied by the adaptable sweet cicely, which is also at home in the deeper and constant shade of the evergreen forest.

The duff and litter under deciduous trees will be quite different in composition, texture, and acidity from that found under pure stands of evergreen fir, spruce, or hemlock. Certain herbaceous and shrubby plants, that are highly sensitive to the nature of the forest litter and the underlying soil, will be very local in occurrence. Many plants respond to small variations in the water table, i.e., to relatively dry or moist conditions, and especially to the amount of drainage resulting from the gradient and the porosity of the subsoil.

The keen observer will detect other factors also, that determine which plant species can be expected in a variety of treed habitats. Some, indeed, are exceedingly local, apparently responding to the micro-climate that may extend over a few square feet. That is one of the reasons why the enthusiasm of the forest wanderer is constantly stimulated.

Plants adapt in different ways to the low light levels of woods and forests. Some, like vanilla leaf and pathfinder plant, respond with very large leaves that are precisely arranged to gather as much as possible of the dim light. The high humidity and absence of wind in such places permit these plants to support thin leaves on long, weak stalks. But other groups of forest plants do not attempt to obtain enough light to synthesize their food from water (of the soil) and carbon dioxide (of the air) with the aid of chlorophyll in green leaves. Instead, like the coral-roots and the Indian pipe, they team with certain fungi in the soil to extract their nourishment from decaying leaves and twigs. Such saprophytic plants are numerous in the coniferous forest, and since they have no need of chlorophyll they show a surprising range of colours—white, or brown, or red, or yellow. Finally, there are a few complete parasites, like the poque or the oak mistletoe, that simply penetrate the living tissues of the host plants by means of special structures (haustoria) through which they absorb the victim's juices.

Dim-light plants sometimes adopt special ways of propagating— due to the absence of bees, the essential plant pollinators of open areas. Many of the species spread (chiefly) by means of runners (like the twin-flower) or of spreading underground rootstocks (like wild lily-of-the-valley). Some—like wild ginger—hold their flowers within reach of other pollinators (such as ants or millipedes), others—like the trilliums and youth-on-age—produce scents that attract small flies (diptera) or beetles. Evergreen violet employs yet another device, for late in the season it may produce closed (or cleistogamous) flowers that never open and are self-fertilized, and so produce viable seed even though the earlier, more showy flowers may not have succeeded in attracting pollinizing insects. Plants that provide parachutes for seed dispersal are seldom found in the windless forest, and are limited to the edges of treed areas. Instead, forest plants often produce (like enchanter's nightshade or sweet cicely) quantities of strongly hooked seeds that may be distributed by passing animals, or hard-coated seeds (concealed in edible berries) that are spread by birds (as is the case with the huckleberries and devil's club). The dwarf mistletoes produce extremely sticky envelopes for their seeds, then in a sudden popping of the turgid fruit project the seeds as much as 12 m (40 ft.) to new host trees, to which they readily cling.

This book contains descriptions of 100 plants one may expect to find during visits to woodlands or forests. The pink fawn lily, which is rather selective in its habitat, will be found here, but the more adaptable (and common) white fawn lily appears in Field Guide 2 (*Wild Flowers of Field and Slope*) because those are its more characteristic homes. Similarly, yellow avalanche lily is to be found in Field Guide 6 (*Wild Flowers of the Mountains*).

In these guide books we have placed the plants within each major environmental association, as far as possible, in the generally accepted Englerian sequence. (This sequence was originally intended to follow the progression of plant development from the primitive and ancient buttercups to the advanced composites.) Minor dislocations from this sequence have been dictated by the necessity of printing vertical and horizontal pictures in pairs. Another advantage in adopting this order is that readers who are accustomed to the arrangement of Engler, will more readily find members of the lily or orchid families (manocotyledons) at the front of the book, those of the (dicotyledonous) pea family near the centre, and of the composite family at the end.

We have stressed common names, since resistance to use of the scientific names has, at least until recently, been widespread. Common names have been fairly well standardized in countries of limited extent that, like England, have a long cultural history. But in so great an area as is covered in these guide books, a bewildering assortment of local names exists for the more common and widespread species. On the other hand, our culture is so young that for many plants, less abundant or more local, no English names have yet been proposed.

So we are faced with the problems, on the one hand—of selection, on the other—of invention. Authorities who have grappled with the latter difficulty (such as M.E. Peck) generally translate the Latin name: thus for *Boykinia elata*—slender boykinia. But for some of the wide-ranging plants it would not be feasible (or even desirable) to list numerous local names. Clearly we should have a generally accepted common name for every plant, just as (with few and decreasing exceptions) we have agreed upon one scientific name for each.

What is *the* common name? We have been guided by the following considerations. Where many local names exist, we have tried to choose the one employed over the largest area, or in some cases, the name of greatest historical significance. Many, but by no means all, of the common names we have given are included in a list of standardized plant names that was prepared by the American Joint Committee on Horticultural Nomenclature. We are not alone, however, in rejecting some of the names proposed, because of the violence done to the English language in run-on names like redosier dogwood, or distressfully for *Spiranthes romanzoffiana*—continental ladiestresses!

The great merit of the Latin names is their universality. Besides, they are often descriptive, and frequently reveal interesting historical details. Grove lover (or grove-lover, or grovelover) is familiar to some English-speaking people, but *Nemophila parviflora* is recognized by persons of every ethnic group. (The name stems from the Greek *nemos*, a grove, and *philein*—to love, from the Latin *parvus*—small or slight, and *flora*—flower.)

We are indebted in very large measure for the taxonomy employed, to Hitchcock, Cronquist, Ownbey, and Thompson in their great five-volume work *Vascular Plants of the Pacific Northwest*. For more northern species we are obligated to definitive studies by Calder and Taylor (*Flora of the Queen Charlotte Islands*) and by Hulten (*Flora of Alaska and Neighboring Territories*), also to the invaluable monographs by Szczawinski, and by T.M.C. Taylor under the aegis of the Provincial Museum, Victoria, BC.

Not included in this series are the trees, or the ferns (for which several excellent illustrated manuals are available), nor the horsetails, grasses, sedges or rushes (which are of interest chiefly to specialists). An effort has been made to include one or more plants that are representative of each of the major flowering plant families,

In the brief descriptions we have used technical terms as little as possible: these few are illustrated in the Glossary at the end of the book.

Dates of flowering have not been given, since they will have wide variance over an area extending across 22° of latitude and perhaps 2,440 m (8000 ft.) of altitude.

When a plant is identified it becomes a known friend. And in a lifetime of happy observation one will constantly discover fresh details about each kind, and add to aesthetic enjoyment the pleasure of discovery.

In the quiet of the wilderness we can sense more readily the relevance of every part of the natural world, and appreciate the role of plants as vital links in the incredibly complex and interdependent chain of life. In the cathedral forest we are brought to realize the need to preserve all of these beautiful life forms, many of them fragile and increasingly subject to hazard. And we reflect that it is needful to make our own individual response to preserve the natural balance of their environment, which is our environment, the environment of all living things.

x 0.7

1. SMALL-FLOWERED FAIRY-BELL, *Prosartes hookeri*, var. *oregana*
(formerly known as *Disporum hookeri*)
In moist shaded areas these parallel-veined leaves are arranged to intercept
as much as possible of the pale light filtering down from the forest canopy.
Each leaf tapers to a drip-tip so that raindrops slip off readily to moisten
the plant's roots. Often the leaves are powdered with pollen from staminate
flowers of conifers (or from maple flowers) high overhead. Petals (3) and
sepals (3) of the pale greenish-white flowers are 13 mm ($^1/_2$ in.) or less,
and distinctly separate or even slightly flared from the base. The 30–60 cm
(1–2 ft.) plants in late summer bear bright ornaments of berries—orange-red
and slightly pointed. Widely distributed in suitable habitats from coast to
Rockies, from central BC to northwest Ore.

x 1.5

2. LARGE-FLOWERED FAIRY-BELL, *Prosartes smithii*
(formerly known as *Disporum smithii*)
Leaves of the fairy-bells are similar, but the flowers of this species are
13–31 mm ($^1/_2$–1$^1/_4$ in.) long, more cream-coloured, and with petals and
sepals forming a cylinder, with only the tips spread outward. Though the
two plants are found together west of the Cascades, from southern BC to
Cal., this is the much rarer species and should be carefully protected. In the
undisturbed cathedral forest these delicate flower-bells ring their soundless
chimes until, as summer wanes, they are replaced by brilliant orange
berries.

x 1.0

3. PINK FAWN LILY, *Erythronium revolutum*
This very beautiful species is found in moist situations, such as river banks
and in moderately shaded open woodland, particularly of deciduous trees.
It prefers sandy humus, and is only locally abundant, from southern BC to
northwestern Cal. The slender roots (corms) perish if the leaves are picked.
Requiring 4–6 years from seed to blooming plant, and never so lovely as in
their natural setting, the thoughtful viewer should appreciate the wisdom of
leaving the flowers for others to admire.

x 1.3

4. FALSE LILY-OF-THE-VALLEY, *Maianthemum dilatatum*
The distinctive pairs of glossy leaves (tapered to drip-tips) often carpet the forest floor, but flowers are usually sparse in such dense colonies. But with more light, along creek banks, most of the plants lift a pale cluster of faintly perfumed blooms. WILD LILY-OF-THE-VALLEY, *M. canadense*, with very much shorter leaf stems (petioles), is found east of the Cascades, Alas. to Cal.

5. SIMPLE-STEMMED TWISTED-STALK, *Streptopus lanceolatus*, var. *curvipes*, (formerly known as *Streptopus roseus*) See **10**
Widely distributed in moist woods throughout our range, to considerable altitudes, this unbranched 30 cm (1 ft.) tall plant is never abundant. The drooping bells are sometimes yellowish, streaked with purple, though usually rose-coloured.

x 0.8

W. Merilees

x 0.2

6. FALSE SOLOMON'S SEAL, *Maianthemum racemosa*
(formerly known as *Smilacina racemosa*)
Clustered leafy shoots of this 60–90 cm (2–3 ft.) plant lift to the dim light
scented panicles of small cream-coloured flowers. Abundant stem leaves
are conspicuously parallel-veined, with drip-tips that indicate the plant's
preference for moist places in woodland or forest edges. Flowers of May
and June give way to berries that become ultimately reddish. Widely distributed on both sides of the Cascades. TRIFOLIATE SOLOMON'S SEAL,
M. trifolium, (formerly known as *S. trifolia)*, is a much smaller plant
(60 cm–3 m/2–10 ft. tall) of cold mossy woods in the northern part of our
range. Its pointed leaves (often 3) clasp the stem and point upwards.

x 0.6

x 0.7

7. STAR-FLOWERED SOLOMON'S SEAL, *Maianthemum stellatum* (formerly known as *Smilacina stellata*)
The 30–60 cm (1–2 ft.) unbranched stems rise from a far-ranging rootstock, so that rather dense colonies are often seen in woodland openings. Flowers appear too small for the large leaves. Green berries are marked at first by 3 purple stripes, which disappear in the mature, dark reddish fruit. Widely distributed and common.

8. HEMLOCK DWARF MISTLETOE, *Arceuthobium tsugense*
"Witches' brooms" and curious swollen stem sections on hemlock and certain other conifers are often caused by this parasitic plant, whose root-like haustoria secure food from the host plant. Inconspicuous 5–10 cm (2–4 in.) yellowish stems produce tiny flowers, then greenish fruits that explosively project the sticky seeds as much as 12 m (40 ft.) to another host. Widespread, Alas. to Mex., coast to Rockies.

x 0.3

W. Merilees

9. LARGE WHITE TRILLIUM, *Trillium ovatum*

This luminous ornament of wood and forest is often in flower by April, hence 'wake robin.' The snowy blooms usually age pinkish, or even purplish. This trillium is protected over its wide range, on both sides of the Cascades, from southern BC to Cal. From Wash. s. on the west side of the Cascades occurs MOTTLED TRILLIUM, *T. chloropetalum,* with leaves mottled with brown, and a narrow-petal flower that is stemless, i.e., grows directly from the junction of the leaves. It is replaced on the eastern side of the Cascades by ROUND-LEAVED TRILLIUM, *T. petiolatum,* with less showy flowers whose yellowish, brownish, or purplish petals remain partly folded. The flower is stemless, carried almost at the ground level, and nearly hidden below the leaves.

x 0.8

10. TWISTED STALK, *Streptopus amplexifolius*
Leaves of this 30–90 cm (1–3 ft.) much-branched plant are easily confused with those of **1** or **2**, but the divisions of the pale greenish-yellow flowers are not simply spreading; they are strongly reflexed. Also each flower hangs from a remarkably kinked slender stalk, which provides a very distinctive recognition feature. The numerous attractive berries are bright red. Found throughout our area from coast to moderate altitudes in the mountains. SMALL TWISTED STALK,*S. streptopoides,* is more subalpine in range, rare, with unbranched zigzag stem 10–20 cm (4–8 in.) tall and rosy flowers that open flat. (Also with rose-coloured flowers that are bell-shaped as **5**.)

x 1.0

11. FAIRY SLIPPER, *Calypso bulbosa* var. *occidentalis*
The goddess daughter of Atlas was Calypso, whose name means *conceal-ment*, with reference to this lovely flower's habit of hiding among the mosses of the forest floor, in the shade—essential to its existence—of high forest trees. The single leaf is firm, oval, corrugated, and over-wintering. The blossom, in the windless air of the forest, delights the wayfarer with its fragrance—fresh, spicy, and utterly distinctive. The tiny "bulb" (corm) is most tenuously fixed to the forest duff by thread-like fibres that are easily broken when the stem is plucked. Since the roots can only obtain nourish-ment with the aid of certain microscopic fungi, the plants do not easily transplant, and should be admired in their native haunts. Range Alas. to Cal., sea level to mid-montane.

x 1.2

J.M. Woollett

12. SPOTTED CORAL-ROOT, *Corallorhiza maculata*
This striking plant of dense woodland is a saprophyte, for its coral-like roots
obtain food—with the aid of certain fungi—from decaying organic matter in
the humus. Hence this, and other saprophytes, need no green colouring
matter (chlorophyll). The smooth fleshy stems are reddish, 10–24 in. (25–60
cm) tall, with a few clasping purplish bracts in place of leaves. The lip of the
flower is white, usually purple-spotted. Sepals and the 2 upper petals are
slightly cupped inward. The yellowish column bears a few tiny purple dots.
Rarely a yellow-flowered form is seen. Range from s. Alas. to Cal.

x 1.1

13. WESTERN CORAL-ROOT, *Corallorhiza mertensiana*
Not quite so northern, and rather more alpine in its range, this 20–50 cm
(8–20 in.) plant is somewhat rarer than **12**. It is found in wet coniferous
forests and along shaded stream banks. Though both subspecies are variable, this plant is distinguished by slim petals and sepals that are widely
spread, an unspotted lip usually purple-flushed, and absence of purple dots
on the taller column. NORTHERN CORAL-ROOT, *C. trifida*, 13–30 cm
(5–12 in.) tall, is widely distributed from Alas. to Cal., but only e. of the
Coast Range. It is the only coral-root with a greenish-yellow (rather than
purplish) stem, and the only one with a white spotted lip divided into
1 large and 2 small lobes.

x 1.2

14. STRIPED CORAL-ROOT, *Corallorhiza striata*
This very showy plant, 30–60 cm (12–24 in.), is at home in dense coniferous (and more rarely deciduous) forest from mid-BC southward. One is some-times fortunate to chance upon a group of these plants in a forest opening, when a shaft of light from behind, like a natural spotlight, transforms the blossoms into coruscating jewels. White (rarely yellow) petals, sepals, and lip are distinctively and vividly striped with purple.

15

16

x 0.4

x 0.5

15. WESTERN RATTLESNAKE PLANTAIN, *Goodyera oblongifolia*
The conspicuous rosette of white-veined, dark green leaves is a striking
feature of the forest floor from Alas. s. to Mexico. (However, the white
may be limited to the mid-vein only.) An unbranched 25–38 cm (10–15 in.)
stem bears about a dozen inconspicuous greenish flowers. NORTHERN
RATTLESNAKE PLANTAIN, *G. repens*, 10–20 cm (4–8 in.), occurs in the
range of **15,** but chiefly e. of the Cascades. Its leaves are often unmarked
and tend to grow *up the stem.*

16. SLENDER-SPIRE ORCHID, *Piperia transversa*
Two to four 10–15 cm (4–6 in.) leaves—thick, smooth-edged, long and
blunt-tipped—arise from the moss or humus in early spring but wither away
before the slender 30–60 cm (1–2 ft.) spire of scented white flowers appears
(late July–Aug.). Range Alas. to Cal., from coast to mountain slopes.

x 0.5

17. ONE-LEAVED REIN-ORCHID,
Platanthera obtusata (formerly *Habenaria obtusata*)
The single 8–13 cm (3–5 in.) blunt-tipped leaf is often partly hidden in the moss of forests, bogs, swamps, or even grassy slopes. Nor is the 15–25 cm (6–10 in.) flower stem, with its greenish-yellow flowers, easily seen. The flower spur is slightly curved, and tapered. The leaf is usually more than twice as long as wide. Range e. of the Cascades from Alas. to n.e. Ore.

x 0.5

x 0.5

18. NORTHWEST TWAYBLADE, *Listera caurina*
This small 10–25 cm (4–10 in.) delicate plant of wet coniferous forests and
boggy mountain slopes is rather rare, and seldom noticed. Two leaves, as in
all twayblades, are held flat about halfway up the thin stem. The flowers are
distinguished by a large lip, unnotched at the tip but with 2 barely visible
spurs at the base. NORTHERN TWAYBLADE, *L. borealis*, is similar, but
its very large lip scarcely tapers from tip to base. Rare and more montane.

19. HEART-LEAVED TWAYBLADE, *Listera cordata*
This 5–20 cm (2–8 in.) slender plant holds its twin leaves above the moss in
bogs and coniferous forests from Alas. to Cal. from sea level to considerable
altitudes. Stem and flowers may be purplish, or in another form, greenish.
Identified by the uniquely forked lip. BROAD-LEAVED TWAYBLADE,
L. convallarioides, (same range) is larger.

x 0.9

x 1.4

W. Merilees

20. SMALL-LEAVED MONTIA, *Montia parvifolia*
From a basal clump of thick egg-shaped 2–3 cm (³/4–1¹/4 in.) leaves, arching stalks, 13–25 cm (5–10 in.) long, support the delicate pink flowers. Very small leaves are alternate (not opposite) up the flower stalk. Range Alas. to Cal., coast to Rockies.

21. HAZELNUT, *Corylus cornuta*
This 1–3.5 m (3–12 ft.) tall shrub, with its large pointed-oval notched leaves occurs from Alas to Cal. from coast to mountain slopes across the continent. The picture shows female flowers (tiny and scarlet, often overlooked). The long male catkins appear Jan.–Feb., before the leaves. Nuts are concealed in green papery husks.

x 0.8

x 1.7

W. Merilees

22. MINER'S LETTUCE, *Claytonia rubra*
This succulent 2.5–30 cm (1–12 in.) plant is easily recognized since the uppermost pair of opposite leaves are joined to form a shallow saucer, from which springs the cluster of small whitish flowers on short slender stalks. Foliage is edible. The 2.5–5 cm (1–2 in.) variety, of open rock ridges, has curiously grey foliage. BC to Cal., coast to lower mountains.

23. SIBERIAN LETTUCE,
Claytonia sibirica
Succulent, pointed elliptical, basal leaves have long stems (petioles) but the 2 opposite leaves of the 5–40 cm (2–16 in.) flower stalks have no petioles, and clasp the stalk. Distinctive is a small bract at the base of each individual flower stem (pedicel). Alas. to Cal from lowland to mid-mountain levels. BLINKS, *Montia linearis*, 2.5–8 cm (1–3 in.), of very wet open places, has narrow thickened leaves and tiny flowers all on one side of the (ultimately) red stems.

x 1.0

x 1.1

24. OAK MISTLETOE, *Phoradendron seropinum ssp. tomentosum*
A serious parasite upon Garry and other oaks, the compact masses of twigs
and greenish-yellow leaves are very noticeable among the oak branches,
especially in winter. Birds are fond of the whitish berries and spread the
sticky-coated seeds. *Phor* (Gk.) = thief, and *dendron* = tree, for this is a
thief of the host's juices. Ore. and N. Cal.

25. SMALL-FLOWERED BUTTERCUP, *Ranunculus uncinatus*
This very common 20–75 cm (8–30 in.) plant of moist places in woods
and forest openings is widespread from Alas. to Cal. The small haphazard
flowers seem quite out of scale for the tall plants. There may be 1–5—rarely
more—pale cream-yellow petals about 3 mm ($1/8$ in.) long. They are succeeded by a ball-head of sharply hooked seeds that hitchhike rides on
passing animals.

x 0.6

26. WILD GINGER, *Asarum caudatum*
The paired heart-shaped glossy leaves of the wild ginger are often found beneath stands of alder or vine maple, but few discover the curious spidery flowers. These may be partly covered by the humus of the forest floor, so are fertilized by small flies, ants, millipedes, and perhaps slugs. The flowers have a faint odour of ginger. The plant occurs from southern BC, s. to Cal. and e. to Montana.

x 0.5

27. BANEBERRY, *Actaea rubra*

The handsome leaves consist of paired and terminal leaflets branching from a central stem (twice-ternate semipinnatifid). They grow from a 60–90 cm (2–3 ft.) branched stem, and are surpassed slightly by rounded clusters of small, fuzzy white flowers. A magnifying glass is needed to distinguish 3–5 sepals, 5–10 slightly longer thread-like petals, and numerous stamens. Fruits are either brilliant red, or in another form, porcelain white—in either case arrestingly attractive, but poisonous. Range Alas. to Cal. and e., in moist woods and along stream banks.

28

29

x 1.0

x 0.3

28. LARGE-LEAVED SANDWORT, *Moeringia macrophylla*
Most sandworts are small tufted plants, of dry sunny sites, with narrow
leaves, but this one prefers shaded woodland, and has thin, broadly
lanceolate leaves in opposite pairs along a weak 5–20 cm (2–8 in.) stem.
Common, BC to Cal., both sides of the Cascades.

29. WOOD ANEMONE, *Anemone deltoidea*
Abundant in woodland and forest, west of the Cascades, Wash. to Cal.,
this delicate 10–25 cm (4–10 in.) plant grows from running rootstocks. A
single basal leaf is divided into 3 notched oval leaflets, similar to those of
the single-flowered stem. As with other anemones, there are no petals, and
the 5 sepals serve the role of petals. They are often bluish-flushed beneath.

x 2.0

30. LYALL'S ANEMONE, *Anemone lyallii*
A most delicate sprite of the woods and forests, this pretty 5–20 cm (2–8 in.) species ranges through s.w. BC to Cal., from coast to Cascades. The 3 tri-leaflet (trifoliate) leaves form a whorl near the top of the fragile stem, which grows from a buff-coloured rootstock (rhizome). The flower is sometimes bluish, or white, though usually pink. There are 12–25 stamens. Very similar is OREGON ANEMONE, *A. oregana*, with (usually) 5 leaflets and a bluish, occasionally pinkish-white flower, having 30–100 stamens. Range Wash. and Ore., mostly e. of the Cascades.

x1.1

31. WESTERN MEADOW RUE, *Thalictrum occidentale*
Tall, 45–100 cm (18–40 in.), and branched, with thin leaves very like those
of columbine, this plant is common in open woodland and along stream
banks, from BC to Cal. on both sides of the Cascades. Male flowers
(illustrated) only are found on one plant, female (pistillate) on another.
FEW-FLOWERED MEADOW RUE, *T. sparsiflorum*, of Alas. BC, Ore.
and Cal., in the Rockies, is similar in leaf and height, but bears perfect
flowers of both sexes on the same plant, unlike the rare and tiny
5–15 cm-high (2–6 in.) alpine MOUNTAIN MEADOW RUE, *T. alpinum*.

x 0.3

x 0.2

32. FALSE BUGBANE, *Trautvetteria caroliniensis*
Wet woodland is often carpeted with the bold basal leaves of this 50–90 cm
(20–36 in.) plant, common also in wet ditches from Alas. to Cal., coast to
Rockies. There are no petals, and the attractiveness of the flower is in the
fluffy head of numerous white stamens that hide the hooked pistils.

33. YOUTH-ON-AGE, *Tolmiea menziesii*
Small buds at the base of the leaf blades develop into aerial "daughter"
plants. Odd greenish-purple tubular flowers are split, and reveal 1 short and
2 long stamens. Leaves are long-stemmed, hairy, and sharply toothed. Moist
woodland and stream banks, Alas. to Cal., coast to Cascades.

x 0.5

34. VANILLA LEAF, *Achlys triphylla*
Forming a solid ground cover in woodland and forest openings, this common
plant ranges from BC to Cal., coast to Cascades. The attractive thin leaves are
unmistakable; bundles of them were formerly dried to scent pioneer kitchens.
Fluffy spikes of flowers yield to sporadic green, then reddish, fruits shaped
like stubby canoes (well worth looking at with a magnifying glass).

x 1.0

35. LONG-LEAVED OREGON GRAPE,

Mahonia nervosa (formerly *Berberis nervosa*)

From spreading rhizomes this very attractive plant produces 10–20 cm (4–8 in.) stems from which rise compound leaves (having 9–19 strongly notched glossy leaflets) and a long cluster (raceme) of pale yellow flowers with stamens that are remarkably sensitive to the slightest touch. The flowers are faintly fragrant, and are succeeded by numerous edible blue berries having a whitish-blue "bloom." Range is from mid-BC to Cal., w. of the Cascades.

36

37

x 0.5

x 1.0

W. Merilees

36. INSIDE-OUT-FLOWER, *Vancouveria hexandra*
Attractive compound leaves, quite like those of **31**, spring from a wide-running rhizome. The extraordinary flowers remind one of pirouetting ballet dancers in white tutus. This delicate woodland plant is found w. of the Cascades from Wash. to Cal. Southern Ore. and Cal. have the beautiful yellow counterpart, YELLOW VANCOUVERIA, *V. chrysantha.*

37. WESTERN CORYDALIS, *Corydalis scouleri*
This rangy plant, 60–120 cm (2–4 ft.), often depends for support, in part, on adjacent plants of wet spots in woodlands and forest openings. The 3 large and handsome compound leaves are topped by long clusters (racemes) of purplish flowers with a lengthy pink spur. The flowers appear inappropriately small for the foliage. Range BC to n. Ore., coast to Cascades.

x 0.7

38. WILD BLEEDING HEART, *Dicentra formosa*
The delicate greyish-green foliage is an attractive and common feature of
moist woods from coast to Cascades, BC to Cal. The dusky-rose flowers
somewhat suggest valentine hearts, each with ribbon bows tied round the
pointed end. DUTCHMAN'S BREECHES, *D. cucullaria*, has similar
foliage growing from a cluster of small rounded tubers, and attractive pink
flowers with bright yellow petal tips. Range eastern Wash. and Ore. Rare
and tiny STEER'S HEAD, *D. uniflora*,, 5–13 cm (2–5 in.), from the
foothills of the Wash. Cascades, e. and s., bears a single white and pink
flower at the top of each stem.

x 0.8

39. TOOTHWORT, *Cardamine nuttallii*
(formerly *Cardamine pulcherrima*)
This pretty pink crucifer blooms in open woodland before leaves of deciduous trees and shrubs obscure the light. Basal leaves with long stalks
(petioles) grow from 2.5–4 cm (1–1^1/$_2$ in.) fleshy rootstocks, and are either
broadly heart-shaped (purplish beneath) with slight notches, or are deeply
divided into irregular lobes. Range is west of the Cascades, BC to Cal.
Very similar is MILK-MAIDS, *C. integrifolia*, w. of Cascades, Ore. and
Cal., growing from a rounded tuber, with usually white flowers. ALPINE
BITTER-CRESS, *C. bellidifolia*, is montane, from Alas. to Cal., with basal
rosette of handsome spoon-shaped leaves, and 2.5–13 cm (1–5 in.) stems
bearing small white 4-petalled flowers followed by very slim-pointed seed
capsules.

x 0.7

40. SLENDER BOYKINIA, *Boykinia occidentalis* (formerly *Boykinia elata*) This attractive 15–60 cm (6–24 in.) plant is not uncommon in moist woods and along stream banks from BC to Cal., coast to Cascades. Leaves may be confused with those of **33** or **44**, but are slightly glossy and distinguished by stem leaves having—at their juncture with the stem—several long, soft, brownish bristles. Petals (5) are pink or whitish flushed with purple.

41. OVAL-LEAVED MITREWORT, *Mitella ovalis* The few long-stemmed, oval, notched, and hairy 2.5–4.5 cm (1–1³/4 in.) leaves are not conspicuous among the other foliage of the forest floor or wet creek banks, and the slim, unbranched, leafless 15–30 cm (6–12 in.) flower stem (scape) bears only tiny greenish flowers, yet this (and other mitreworts)—on examination with a magnifying glass—reveal hidden beauty. This species is common from BC to Cal., coast to Cascades.

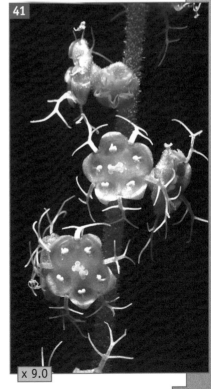

x 9.0

x 0.8

42. FEATHERY MITREWORT, *Mitella breweri*
All the mitreworts have a few hairy, somewhat roundish but variously
notched, basal leaves—always with long white-haired stalks (petioles).
All have slender unbranched flower stems (scapes), 15–40 cm (6–16 in.)
tall, that are leafless (except in LEAFY-STEMMED MITREWWORT,
M. caulescens, which has 2–3 small stem leaves). And all have tiny flowers,
like exquisitely crafted wire jewellery in green or yellow gold. This species is
distinguished by very rounded leaves 4–8 cm (1^{1}/2–3 in.) broad, and by its
thread-like petals that *alternate* with the 5 stamens. Range BC to Cal., in
moist alpine woods (to treeline).

x 5.0

43. ALPINE MITREWORT, *Mitella pentandra*
This delicate inhabitant of moist and shaded places in the mountains
(from Alas. to Cal.) must be closely examined if its miniature beauty is to be
discovered. The 5 yellow petals, branched and thread-like, arise from the
flattened basal flower platform (hypanthium) directly *opposite* each of the 5
stamens. Basal leaves are very like those of **41**. NORTHERN MITREWORT,
M. nuda, Alas. to n.w. Wash, 5–20 cm (2–8 in.) tall, is distinguished by 10
stamens, and 5 greenish-yellow petals. White petals tinged with lavender,
with 3 lobes and less like skeletons, make THREE-TOOTHED MITRE-
WORT, *M. trifida*, easily recognizable. BC to Cal., in Cascades and
Olympics.

x 0.7

x 1.2

44. TALL FRINGE-CUP, *Tellima grandiflora*
Clustered basal leaves are 2.5–8 cm (1–3 in.) broad, kidney-shaped, hairy
and coarse-toothed, with long stalks (petioles). Short-petioled, reduced
leaves grow along the unbranched flower stems (scapes). Stamens (10). The
ragged skeleton petals age pinkish, and regions of purple often outline leaf
mid-ribs. Woodlands Alas. to Cal., coast to Selkirks.

45. FALSE MITREWORT, *Tiarella trifoliata* var. *laciniata*
The dainty "foam flowers" of the 3 species of *Tiarella* appear usually in
threes on 20–38 cm (8–15 in.) stems that bear reduced leaves, similar to the
longer-stalked basal leaves. These are deeply 3 to 5-cleft and sharply
notched, but 3-lobed in almost identical LACEFLOWER, *T. trifoliata*, and
only notched in SUGAR-SCOOP, *T. trifoliata* var. *unifoliata*, so named
because one of the 5 sepals is enlarged and resembles a sugar scoop. All are
widely distributed throughout our area.

x 1.5

x 0.5

46. PURPLE PEA,
Lathyrus nevadensis
The 20–50 cm (8–30 in.) plants are
often nearly free-standing, though the
leaves are tipped with once-forked
tendrils. Stems are angled, but not
winged. Leaves have 4–10 paired or
scattered leaflets that end in short
points (mucronate). Tip of pistil hairy
on lower side only, like a toothbrush
(cf. the vetches **52, 53, 54**). Common
and variable, BC to Cal.

47. COAST TRAILING CURRANT,
Ribes laxiflorum
Most of the numerous species of
currants (spineless) and gooseberries
(with spines) are found on open slopes,
but this one prefers wet woods, from
Alas. to Cal. The weak unarmed
branches (with reddish-brown bark)
may sprawl to 6 m (20 ft.) over other
shrubs. Leaves are 8–10 cm (3–4 in.)
broad and sprinkled with transparent
dots (glands). Berries are reddish-
brown, hairy, and unpalatable.

x 0.3

x 0.2

W. Merilees

48. LARGE-LEAVED AVENS, *Geum macrophyllum*

Common, 30–90 cm (12–36 in.), in moist woods and on stream banks, Alas. to Cal. coastal to montane. The large curved and hooked seeds (achenes) from the ball-head of seeds frequently accumulate on pant legs and stockings. Basal leaves, 30–40 cm (12–16 in.) long, have oddly assorted leaflets along the stalk (rachis), and a very large terminal notched leaflet up to 13 cm (5 in.) wide.

49. CREEPING RASPBERRY, *Rubus pedatus*

From Alas. to Cal., coast to Rockies, this attractive unarmed creeping raspberry is found in wet woodland. Strung together by thin wiry stolons (runners), each plant has 2–3 shining leaves and a single flower with 4 down-turned sepals and 5 white petals. Fruit has only 1–3 reddish drupelets, but is sweet-flavoured.

x 0.7

50. OSOBERRY, *Oemleria cerasiformis*
(formerly *Osmaronia cerasiformis*)
In open woods and stream banks this 2–3 m (6–10 ft.) shrub opens its
flowers as early as Feb., from BC to Cal., coast to Cascades. The flowers
(and foliage) are strong smelling, some say like crushed cucumber, but
perhaps most like spring and burgeoning growth. A close look is needed to
discover that some flowers are staminate (with 3 ranks of about 5 stamens
each), others pistillate (with 5 pistils and shorter stamens, whose anthers
never mature). The bitter fruit is a very attractive bright orange 13 mm
($1/2$ in.) plum, but seldom ripens to purple because it is so sought by birds.

x 1.0

51. DWARF WOODLAND ROSE, *Rosa gymnocarpa*
The specific name refers to the fact, distinctive of this species among the roses of our area, that the little vase-shaped scarlet hips are *bare*, having shed their crown of short sepals. This delightful small bush, 60–120 cm (2–4 ft.), spreads its dainty pink flowers in coastal to low-montane woodland from s. BC to Cal., chiefly w. of the Cascades. Twigs are variably bristly to almost unarmed; flowers are 2–2.5 cm (³/4–1 in.) broad. PRICKLY ROSE, *R. acicularis*, is another small-flowered, 2.5–5 cm (1–2 in.), rose of wooded regions of Alas. and BC, with twigs armed with many short straight thorns. Its dark purple hips are crowned with persisting short sepals.

x 0.5

x 0.9

52. WILD VETCH, *Vicia americana*
This variable and widely distributed (Alas. to Mex., coast to mid-continent) climbing vetch, 105 cm (3¹/₂ ft.), has 8–12 leaflets, and well-developed tendrils. Flower clusters are borne on definite flower stems (peduncles). Some varieties have narrow short-haired leaflets, others wider hairless leaflets.

53. COMMON VETCH, *Vicia sativa ssp. nigra*
This immigrant species is now found across the continent, from BC south-ward. Like all vetches, it is distinguished from peas by the "bottle brush" style (central portion of pistil), i.e., the hairs are arranged all around. A variable annual, with 8–14 leaflets (each ending in a short projection of the mid-rib), this has branched tendrils. Flowers (2–3), found between leaf stalk and main stem, lack stalks (pedicels).

x 1.0

x 2.0

W. Merilees

54. HAIRY VETCH, *Vicia hirsuta*

This small, 30–60 cm (12–24 in.), clambering annual has very small white to palest lavender flowers on definite stalks (pedicels). Leaflets (14–18) are squared off at the ends (except for a minute projection of the mid-vein). Pod is downy, with (usually) 2 seeds. Now widely distributed in woodland and pasture, BC to Ore.

55. WOOD SORREL, *Oxalis oregana*

Moist woods from coast to Cascades, Wash. to Cal., are in some places carpeted with the attractive "shamrock" leaves and *single* pink, darker-veined flowers. GREAT OXALIS, *O. trilliifolia*, is similar in leaf and range, but the smaller flowers occur in clusters of 3–7. YELLOW WOOD SORREL, *O. stricta*, is widespread and has smaller yellow flowers.

x 1.0

x 0.9

56. FALSE BOX, *Paxistima myrsinites* (formerly *Pachistima myrsinites*)
This very handsome evergreen shrub, 60–152 cm (2–5 ft.), of BC to Cal.,
coast to Rockies, is endangered near cities because the attractive glossy
foliage is collected, by the ton, for the florists' trade. The 4-petalled
mahogany red flowers are pleasantly scented. Small beaked capsules are
brown, and rarely noticed.

57. ENCHANTER'S NIGHTSHADE, *Circaea alpina*
Possibly in this case the enchantment resides largely in the name, for the
variable plant, in either form, is visually insignificant. It occurs in cool damp
woods and along gravel stream bars from Cal. northward and eastward. The
white-flowered form, 15–45 cm (6–18 in.) tall (illustrated), is replaced on
river bars by a compact 4–10 cm (2–4 in.) form with fleshy leaves and larger
pink-flushed flowers. Both forms have small hook-covered fruits.

x 1.8

x 0.3

58. YELLOW WOOD VIOLET, *Viola glabella*
This very common 15–30 cm (6–12 in.) plant often occurs in extensive
stands in moist open woods, from Alas. to Cal. Upper third of the succulent
stem bears 5–8 cm (2–3 in.) smooth, heart-shaped, serrate leaves. Flowers
are very short-spurred with tip of pistil and inner part of the two lateral
petals white-bearded. Lower petal is always well isolated from the other
four.

59. WILD SARSAPARILLA, *Aralia nudicaulis*
The single, large, triple-compound leaf of this unusual plant is conspicuous
in certain woodlands of e. BC and Wash. The leaflets are held parallel to
the ground, at the top of a 30–50 cm (12–20 in.) leaf stalk, and quite hide
the obscure triple ball-shaped clusters of tiny greenish flowers. These
produce purple berries. The plants spread by wide-running rhizomes,
which are pleasantly scented.

x 1.8

60. EVERGREEN VIOLET, *Viola sempervirens*
This attractive and widespread species (BC to Cal., coast to Cascades)
spreads by creeping stems over the floor of moist woods. Leaves are evergreen, firm and broadly heart-shaped, springing from a common origin with
the leafless flower stems, which are 5–10 cm (2–4 in.) tall. Brown or purple
dots usually appear on the underside of the older leaves. Flowers are very
short spurred. CANADA VIOLET, *V. canadensis*, inhabits woodland from
Alas. to Ore, e. to the Rockies and beyond. Its petals are white, with yellow
bases (but the back faces are purplish) and the 2 lateral petals are bearded,
the 3 lower pencilled with purple lines ("honey guides" to insects). Plant is
similar to **58**, but the leaves are more pointed.

x 0.4

61. DEVIL'S CLUB, *Oplopanax horridus*

The enormous, 40 cm (16 in.), broad leaves, with yellowish spines lining
the veins of the lower surface, are quite unmistakable. These armed leaves
and the even more viciously spined, 1.2–3 m (4–10 ft.) springy stems are
known to every hiker in the wet coastal forest, for the scratches they inflict
usually become sore and inflamed. The small flowers occur in large clusters,
and have 5 each of tiny sepals, greenish-white petals, and stamens, plus the
2 styles. The handsome berries are sealing-wax red. Range Alas. to Cal., and
e. to Mont.

62

x 0.5

63

x 0.6

62. SWEET CICELY,
Osmorhiza berteroi (formerly known as *Osmorhiza chilensis*)
This thin-leaved 30–90 cm (1–3 ft.) perennial is abundant in forest and woodland from Alas. to Cal. The much-branched, more or less hairy stems lift compound leaves to the faint light, at first with long stalks that become shorter upward. The tiny flowers yield to bristly spear-shaped fruits 1.25–2 cm (1/2–3/4 in.) long.

63. GREENISH-FLOWERED PYROLA, *Pyrola virens*
The small 10–20 cm (4–8 in.) stem and greenish flowers rise above thick, oval leaves, 1.25–2.5 cm (1/2–1 in.) long, in coniferous forests from Alas. to Cal., usually though not invariably east of the Cascades. Flowers (3–10) grow all around the tip of the stem (unlike those of **68**).

x 0.2

64. PACIFIC DOGWOOD, *Cornus nuttallii*
Among the world's finest flowering trees, at 18 m (60 ft.), this floral emblem
of British Columbia is also found southward to California, w. of the
Cascades. Breathtaking in May and June—when decked with thousands of
13–18 cm (5–7 in.) cream-coloured blossoms—the splendid trees are arrest-
ing again in Sept. and Oct. when the heavily veined, wavy-edged leaves
turn a harmonious blend of plum purple, pink and even rose. At the same
time (the creamy bracts having fallen) the (true) flower heads are replaced
by clusters of drupes, all brilliant scarlet barbarically edged with orange.
Then the tree is, indeed, incredibly beautiful.

x 1.0

65. SINGLE DELIGHT, *Moneses uniflora*
This elegant nymph prefers moist areas, where much rotting wood is incorporated in the soil. Its one charming bloom hangs demurely from the top of a short, 2.5–15 cm (1–6 in.), slender stem, in woodlands from coast to Rockies, and from Alas. to Cal. The handsome leaves (sometimes entire-edged) are chiefly basal. Unlike the related pyrolas, 'single delight' holds its waxen-white petals flat, or slightly reflexed, and is centred by a unique pistil that is reminiscent of a chess piece—the castle or rook. Very choice and delicate, this lovely plant should be left undisturbed in its natural haunts.

x 0.6

66. LARGE WINTERGREEN, *Pyrola asarifolia*
Very showy is this ubiquitous plant, found throughout western US and most of Canada. Its handsome "shiny leaves," egg- to heart-shaped, leathery, and glossy dark-green (often purplish beneath), are found in moist, shaded ground. The 15–40 cm (6–16 in.) flower stem is unbranched, and carries 10–24 waxy pink to purplish flowers. Flowers are structurally similar to those of **63** but very different in colour. LESSER WINTERGREEN, *P. minor*, only 10–18 cm (4–7 in.) tall, is much like **66** but with a shorter, straight pistil. Alas. to Cal., coast to Rockies.

x 0.6

x 0.6

67. WHITE-VEINED PYROLA, *Pyrola picta*
Handsome thick leaves "painted" with white veins (and usually purplish beneath) distinguish this attractive species, which has yellowish to greenish-white (rarely purplish) flowers. Found in coniferous forests from Alas. to Cal., coast to Rockies. ARCTIC WINTERGREEN, *P. grandiflora*, of montane woods, Alas. to n. BC, has notably large white flowers, pink-tinged and very beautiful, and very leathery leaves that are often whitened along the veins.

68. ONE-SIDED PYROLA, *Orthilia secunda*
This very common species, 5–15 cm (2–6 in.) tall, has all of its 6–20 greenish-white flowers on one side of the flower stem (hence "second") and its small 2–5 cm ($3/4$–2 in.) leaves grow *up the stem*, unlike the other pyrolas. Alas. to Cal., coast to Rockies and beyond.

x 0.5

69. CANDY-STICK, *Allotropa virgata*
The common name is descriptive of this spectacular 10–40 cm (4–16 in.) saprophytic plant. Stiff, bright red stems carry numerous flowers with 5 white or pink sepals, 10 purplish stamens, and a 5-lobed pistil and stigma. Leaves are replaced by slim, pointed, white bracts, since the plant (drawing its nourishment from decaying organic matter of the forest floor) does not need, nor produce, chlorophyll. Not uncommon at lower elevations, BC to Cal., coast to Cascades.

x 1.0

70. GNOME PLANT,
Hemitomes congestum
Very curious, and quite rare, is
this saprophytic plant of dense
coniferous forests of the coastal
regions from BC to Cal.
Yellowish to bright pink, the
2.5 cm (1 in.) plants, at first like
small cauliflower heads, elon-
gate sometimes to 18 cm (7 in.)
as they mature. Sepals and
petals (5 each) are similar in
colour, and soft-haired within.

71. LITTLE PRINCE'S PINE,
Chimaphila menziesii
This attractive lesser brother of
75 has smaller, darker green, less
waxy leaves that are elliptical
and saw-edged. The rather
sprawling stem seldom rises
more than 10 cm (4 in.) above
the moss of forest floors. Flesh-
coloured flowers are often solitary, less often 2–3, rarely up to
8. Range s. BC especially
coastal, to Cal.

71

x 0.7

x 1.0

72. PINE-SAP, *Monotropa hypopitys*
Yellowish, orange, less often pinkish, this saprophytic plant is of wide
occurrence in the humus of dark forests from BC to Cal., and eastward.
"Pine-sap" calls attention to the odd plant's preference for pine (and other
conifers) and to the shape and colour, which suggest congealed drippings of
pine resin. The flowers tend to grow on one side only of the curved stem
(which straightens, and lengthens to 25 cm (10 in.) as the seed capsules
mature). Resembles **73**, but the flowers are coloured and several, rather
than colourless and solitary, on each stem.

x 0.9

73. INDIAN PIPE, *Monotropa uniflora*
Total absence of green colouring matter (chlorophyll) declares this extraordinary 5–25 cm (2–10 in.) plant a saprophyte, which obtains its nourish-
ment (with the aid of certain fungi) from decaying vegetable matter. The
white, often clustered stems, in the deep gloom of coniferous forests, attract
much interest. The single spectral flower nods at first—like a pipe with the
bowl turned down against the rain—but as the seeds mature and the plant
turns black, the capsules face upward. Range Alas. to Cal., e. to the
Atlantic. FRINGED PINE-SAP, *Pleuricospora fimbriolata* barely lifts its
upward-facing, whitish to brownish clustered flowers above the forest duff,
in the Olympics, s. to Cal. The corolla is *not* densely hairy within, unlike **72**.

x 0.3

74. PINE-DROPS, *Pterospora andromedea*
This is by far the tallest of the saprophytes, with stately brown and sticky
stems reaching 1 m (3 ft.). Often unobserved, since the brown colour
blends with the forest floor, this unique plant ranges from Alas. to Cal.,
coast to Rockies. The numerous hanging flowers are yellowish, with stalks
(pedicels) and 5-parted calyx reddish. They mature to brown capsules that
release enormous numbers of extraordinary seeds, each semi-collared by a
diaphanous "sail." The dead woody stems often remain standing through a
second, and even a third winter.

x 0.5

W. Merilees

75. PIPSISSEWA, *Chimaphila umbellata*

Chimaphila—from Gk. *cheima* = winter, and *philos* = loving—is nicely descriptive of this beautiful evergreen plant, whose sturdy foliage positively revels in rain, or even snow. The remarkable pink flowers nod, each at the end of a short curved stalk, from a smooth 10–25 cm (4–10 in.) stem. The stem bears 1 or 2 whorls of thick leaves, wax-glossed and conspicuously saw-toothed. If the 5-petalled 2.5 cm-wide (1 in.) flower is turned up, one sees 10 curiously shaped stamens that radiate, like wheel spokes, around the huge hub of the fat green ovary. Range: forests of Alas. to Cal., coast to Rockies.

x 0.7

x 2.5

W. Merilees

76. COPPER BUSH, *Elliottia pyroliflora*
(formerly *Cladothamnus pyroliflorus*)
This is an unusually flowered 60 cm–2 m (2–7 ft.) shrub of cool, shaded, subalpine forests from Alas. to n.w. Ore., west of the Cascades. Leaves are pale green and unnotched. The 4 cm (1¹/₂ in.) flowers are solitary, borne near the ends of the branches, copper to salmon-coloured, and distinguished by a remarkably large curved pistil.

77. RED HUCKLEBERRY, *Vaccinium parvifolium*
One of the brightest accents of the sombre forest is provided by the bright cerise-red fruit, glowing and semi-translucent, of this attractive, 1–2.4 m (3–8 ft.) shrub. Its pale green, strongly angled stems, clothed with small leaves and bright pink buds, bear single, inconspicuous pinkish-yellow, globular flowers. Range: Alas. to Cal., w. of the Cascades.

x 1.0

W. Merilees

78. WESTERN TEA-BERRY, *Gaultheria ovatifolia*
This flat-growing, shrubby plant is smaller in all its parts, but clearly related
to **79**. It is a most attractive plant, and exceptionally wide-ranging, from
open ponderosa pine stands, under scrub conifers at higher altitudes, to
cold bogs and subalpine stony slopes. The 2.5–4 cm (1–1½ in.), glossy and
firmly textured, evergreen leaves have finely saw-toothed margins, and are
paler beneath. Small pink campanulate flowers, with flared corolla lobes,
appear singly in the axils of the leaves. The fruit remains bright and firm for
several months. Range: BC to Cal., coast to Rockies.

x 0.4

x 0.4

W. Merilees

79. SALAL, *Gaultheria shallon*
The handsome evergreen foliage is familiar in coniferous forests, thickets, and even on spray-swept shores. Though commonly 1–3 ft. (30–90 cm) high, we have seen (on the west coast of Vancouver I.) the woody branches struggle up through 6 m (20 ft.) of crisscrossed fallen trees. The edible blue-black fruit is abundant and—dried and pounded into flat cakes—was an important food for First Nations and early explorers. Range of this fine shrub is w. of the Cascades, BC to Cal.

80. FALSE AZALEA, *Menziesia ferruginea*
Moist woods at higher levels and mountain stream banks are home to this 60–180 cm (2–6 ft.) bush, with thin, hairy, 5–6 cm (2–2 1/2 in.) leaves that are much paler beneath, and become brilliant orange and crimson in the fall. The copper-coloured bell flower is scarcely 13 mm (1/2 in.) long. Alas. to Cal.

x 1.2

W. Merilees

x 0.7

J.M. Woollett

81. BLACK HUCKLEBERRY, *Vaccinium membranaceum*
This 60–180 cm (2–6 ft.) spreading shrub is common on forested mountain slopes, from BC to Cal., coast to Rockies. Ovate leaves are thin, 2.5–5 cm (1–2 in.) long, with pointed tips. Single creamy-pink flowers soon are replaced by deep purplish-black berries that become as much as 13 mm (1/2 in.) in diameter. This fruit is a favourite with hikers.

82. EVERGREEN HUCKLEBERRY, *Vaccinium ovatum*
This very handsome 60–245 cm (2–8 ft.) evergreen shrub is found in openings of coniferous forests from BC to Cal., w. of the Cascades. The leathery oval leaves are disposed in flat planes, and contrast with the apricot colour of young leaves. Pink flowers hang in clusters of 3–10. The small fruit is abundant, and resembles black shot; though edible, it is not so bland as that of **81**.

x 0.6

83. STARFLOWER, *Trientalis latifolia*

These pretty little sprites make a delightful pattern on the forest floor, especially around the edges of natural openings. Fragile and dainty above their ring of delicate green leaves, the pale pink (to whitish) flowers beguile the eye. Round white seed cases are uniquely marked and exactly resemble tiny "soccer balls." Edible starchy roots (tubers) are placed vertically in the forest duff. Range s. BC to Cal., chiefly w. of Cascades. NORTHERN STARFLOWER, *T. europaea ssp. arctica*, carries its smaller leaves up the stem (not in a ring near the top), and its tubers are horizontal. Flowers are usually white. Found in shaded bogs and swamps, BC to Ore., w. of Cascades.

x 0.5

x 1.0

84. SLENDER WATERLEAF, *Hydrophyllum tenuipes*
Moist woodlands from coast to Cascades, from s. BC to Cal., are the home
of this 50–90 cm (2–3 ft.) plant. Both basal and stem leaves are large—up to
15 cm (6 in.) broad—and attract more attention than the rather dowdy
flowers, which may be cream, greenish-white, or purplish. Most noticeable
are the 5 long, protruding stamens.

85. YERBA BUENA, *Satureja douglasii*
This little evergreen trailing mint of shaded woods, is valued for the
aromatic scent of its crushed leaves. The long, tough, creeping stems may
be a metre long and root at the internodes. Slightly glossy leaves are about
2.5 cm (1 in.) long, variably toothed, and opposite. Pale lavender-pink
flowers fade white, and are notable for 2 unequal pairs of stamens with
dark crimson anthers. Range: s.w. BC to Cal., coast to Cascades.

x 2.0

86. GROVE LOVER,
Nemophila parviflora
This small insignificant weak-stemmed plant sprawls through other supporting plants in shaded woods and thickets from BC to Cal. LARGE FLOWERED NEMOPHILA, *N. menziesii* (annual), has beautiful, flat (salverform) flowers—bright blue, or sometimes white, veined with lavender, spotted dark blue. Plants are 8–15 cm (3–6 in.), rather sprawling, with opposite, succulent leaves (like **86**). Ore. and Cal.

87. ROUND-LEAVED
SYNTHYRIS, *Synthyris reniformis*
This familiar low plant of coniferous woods, from s.w. Wash. to Cal. w. of Cascades, has clustered long-stalked handsome leaves barely exceeded by leafless flower stems (scapes). Purplish bell-shaped flowers are in a small cluster. MOUNTAIN SYN-THYRIS, *S. schizantha* of shaded ledges in the Olympics and Cascades of Wash. and Ore., has flatter, curiously fringed flowers in a longer cluster.

W. Merilees

x 1.0

x 0.2

x 1.0

88. LEAFY LOUSEWORT, *Pedicularis racemosa*
This 15–45 cm (6–18 in.) weak-stemmed plant bears very odd, washed-out looking whitish flowers in the axils of the numerous leaves. Leaves are long-oblong (2–3), and doubly saw-toothed. The strangely disorganized and asymmetric flowers are often twisted upside down, and the lip (galea) is hooked like a claw and deflected to one side. Coniferous woods in the mountains, BC to Cal.

89. POQUE, *Boschniakia hookeri*
Sharp eyes are needed to mark this strange, 5–13 cm (2–5 in.) plant, among similarly coloured duff of the forest floor (from Alas. to Cal., near the coast). There are 2 colour phases, occasionally seen parasitizing the same root (stolon) of the salal, its usual host. First Nations used the plant for food; though substantial, it scarcely looks appetizing, and in fact, resembles a Douglas fir cone placed upright.

x 1.0

90. TWIN-FLOWER, *Linnaea borealis*
This exquisite small plant spreads long runners creeping over the moss, or trailing from rotting logs or stumps. From the runners, at frequent intervals, rise 5–10 cm (2–4 in.) stems that fork at the top to support two slender trumpets, demure, perfumed, pink and rose-flushed. Where a patch of sunlight reaches the forest floor, an elfin troupe of these little flowers fills the air with an incredible sweetness—surely one of the most enchanting of all plant fragrances. Fortunately, it is widespread, even abundant, from Cal. to Alas., and around the pole to China, northern Europe, and even Greenland.

x 0.5

92

x 0.4

91. ORANGE HONEYSUCKLE,
Lonicera ciliosa
This showy but unscented vine
climbs shrubs and trees, in woodlands and forest openings, from
sea level to the Cascade mountain
slopes, s. BC to n. Cal. Quite
frequently young Douglas firs are
so weakened by the tight coils of
this vine that they break under the
pressure of wind or snow.

92. TARWEED, *Madia sativa*
Almost invariably companion of
98, in dry woods, this very sticky
20–75 cm (8–30 in.) erect plant
also occurs along roadsides from
BC to Cal., w. of the Cascades,
and curiously, also in Chile.
Strongly scented (perhaps of
rhubarb rather than tar). Ray-
flowers look dispirited, since they
open first at night. Seeds are oily,
and were collected for food by
California Natives. SHOWY
TARWEED, *M. elegans*, has larger
yellow flowers, and seeks more
open roadsides.

x 0.8

x 1.3

93. PURPLE HONEYSUCKLE, *Lonicera hispidula*
Never achieving the length of **91**, this climber shares with that species the peculiarity that the uppermost pair of leaves is joined along the base to form a shallow cup. Distinctive of this species is a pair of conjoined stipules, looking like 2 small ears on the stem, from which point the short stalks of the lower leaves grow. Thickets and woods, s. BC to Cal., w. of Cascades.

94. SNOWBERRY, *Symphoricarpos albus*
Common in woods and thickets, Alas. to Cal. and eastward, this thin-branched 1–1.8 m (3–6 ft.) shrub is recognized at once by its abundant wax-white berries. Clusters of pink bell-shaped flowers are faintly perfumed. Nearly related, more dwarf species occur in the mountains, but CREEPING SNOWBERRY, *S. mollis*, is distinctive in its low habit and has broader flowers, less hairy within. Range is similar.

x 2.0

95. SCOULER'S HAREBELL, *Campanula scouleri*
This charming but unobtrusive 8–25 cm (3–10 in.) harebell, or hairbell, is
found in woodland from Alas. to Cal., chiefly w. of the Cascades. The
smooth and alternate leaves are at first long-stalked and round-bladed, but
upward are shaped like arrowheads and are without stalks (petioles). The
flowers are lavender—so pale as to appear nearly white. The corolla is a
wide 13 mm (1/2 in.) bell, and the pistil a very long clapper.

96

x 0.1

97

x 0.4

96. PATHFINDER PLANT, *Adenocaulon bicolor*
There is a sharp contrast between the green upper and white lower surfaces of the large 10–15 cm (4–6 in.) leaves, so that as strollers in semi-shaded wood look behind, they see their trail marked by the white pattern of leaves they have disturbed. The 30–90 cm (1–3 ft.) stem branches above to insignificant "flower heads," actually containing numerous tiny staminate and distinct pistillate flowers. Range s. BC to Cal.

97. SHOWY ASTER, *Aster conspicuus*
Conspicuous is this fine aster, when in late July or August, its handsome blooms dominate open woodland in the mountains. The very large ovate leaves, to 15 cm (6 in.), are generally saw-toothed, and grow directly from the erect stem, i.e., they have no stalks (petioles). The flower heads may span 5 cm (2 in), the ray-florets numbering 12–36. Common: Yukon through BC to n.e. Ore.

x 0.3

x 0.3

98. WHITE-FLOWERED HAWKWEED, *Hieracium albiflorum*
These 30–75 cm (12–30 in.) plants are abundant in open woods, coast to
Rockies, from BC to Cal. Stems bear long white hairs below, but are nearly
smooth upward. Tufted basal leaves and those low on the stem have short
stalks, upper smaller leaves clasp the stem. The bracts that clasp the flower
head (involucre) are blackish-green. Often occurs with **92**.

99. NIPPLEWORT, *Lapsana communis*
This European weed is now common in fields, less so in woodland, chiefly
w. of the Cascades, from Alas. southward. The single erect, variably hairy,
30–150 cm (1–5 ft.) stem carries several thin, 5–13 cm (2–5 in.), wavy-edged
leaves. Lower stalked leaves resemble banjos, but upper leaves have mini-
mal stalks (petioles). Generally 8 green bracts surround each flower head.

x 0.7

100. SPEAR-HEAD SENECIO, *Senecio triangularis*
This bold plant of woodland openings may attain 1.8 or even 2 m (6–7 ft.)
in the rich soil of river banks. It is smooth throughout, with strong, sometimes striated stems carrying large, 23 cm (9 in.) long, triangular leaves that
are unmistakable. Lower leaves are strikingly notched, with squared-off
base and lengthy stalk, the upper saw-toothed and slimmer, without stalk
(petiole). Somewhat ragged ray-florets usually total 8, or less. Alas. to Cal.
These make this distinctive from other species of groundsel, e.g., WOOD
GROUNDSEL, *S. sylvaticus* and COMMON GROUNDSEL, *S. vulgaris*
in which the rayflorets are very much reduced.

Index

Glossary

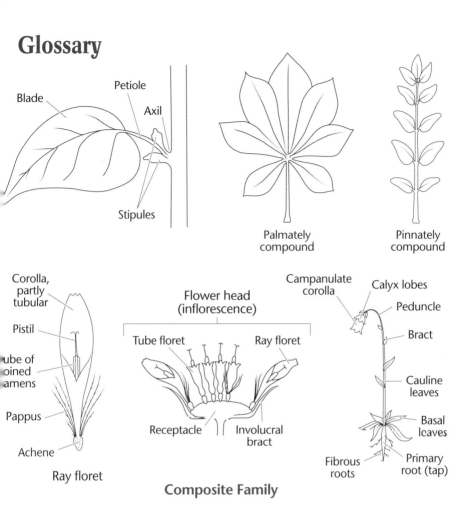

Blade
Petiole
Axil
Stipules

Palmately compound

Pinnately compound

Corolla, partly tubular
Pistil
ube of oined amens
Pappus
Achene

Ray floret

Flower head (inflorescence)
Tube floret
Ray floret
Receptacle
Involucral bract

Composite Family

Campanulate corolla
Calyx lobes
Peduncle
Bract
Cauline leaves
Basal leaves
Primary root (tap)
Fibrous roots

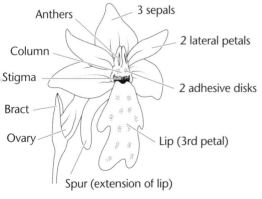

Anthers
3 sepals
2 lateral petals
Column
Stigma
2 adhesive disks
Bract
Ovary
Lip (3rd petal)
Spur (extension of lip)

Orchid Family

Scale

Figures in white inside each picture in the book indicate the scale of the reproduction, e.g. x 0.5 means the picture is half as large as the actual (average) plant; x 2.0 means the picture is twice as large as the plant.

Additional Field Guides from Harbour Publishing

Whelks to Whales: Coastal Marine Life of the Pacific Northwest by Rick M. Harbo
5.5" x 8.5" • 248 pages, 500 colour photos • 1-55017-183-6 • $24.95
This full-colour field guide to the marine life of coastal British Columbia, Alaska, Washington, Oregon and northern California is perfect for divers, boaters, beachwalkers and snorkellers.

Shells and Shellfish of the Pacific Northwest by Rick M. Harbo
5.5" x 8.5" • 272 pages, 350 colour photos • 1-55017-146-1 • $24.95
This easy-to-follow, full-colour guide introduces more than 250 species of mollusks found alon the beaches and shallow waters of the Pacific Northwest.

Coastal Fishes of the Pacific Northwest by Andy Lamb and Phil Edgell
5.5" x 8.5" • 224 pages, 175 colour photos • 0-920080-75-8 • $21.95
The only comprehensive field guide to marine fishes of BC, Washington and southern Alaska.

Lake, River and Sea-Run Fishes of Canada by Frederick H. Wooding
6" x 9" • 304 pages, 50 colour illustrations and line drawings • 1-55017-175-5 • $18.95 paper
The only popular guide to freshwater fishes in all parts of Canada.

Whales of the West Coast by David E. Spalding
6" x 9" • 211 pages, 100 photos • 1-55017-199-2 • $18.95 paper
Everything you need to know about whales and dolphins of the West Coast. David Spalding brings his forty years as a naturalist to this comprehensive look at all the whales that live in Pacific Northwest waters, from the better-known orcas, grays and humpbacks to porpoises, blu whales and sperm whales.

The Beachcomber's Guide to Seashore Life in the Pacific Northwest by J. Duane Sept
5.5" x 8.5" • 240 pages, 500 colour photos • 1-55017-204-2 • $21.95
274 of the most common animals and plants found along the saltwater shores of the Pacific Northwest are described in this book. Illustrating each entry is a colour photo of the species in its natural habitat.

Pacific Seaweeds: A Guide to Common Seaweeds of the West Coast by Louis Druehl
5.5" x 8.5" • 190 pages, 80 colour photos, illustrations • 1-55017-240-9 • $24.95
The authoritative guide to over 100 common species of seaweed. Includes interesting facts, sci-entific information and tasty recipes.

West Coast Fossils by Rolf Ludvigsen and Graham Beard
5.5" x 8.5" • 216 pages, 250 photos, illustrations and maps • 1-55017-179-8 • $18.95
This complete new and expanded edition of a West Coast classic is a concise and thorough guide to the small and large fossils of Vancouver Island and the Gulf Islands of Canada.